Feng Shui
Fundamentals

Love

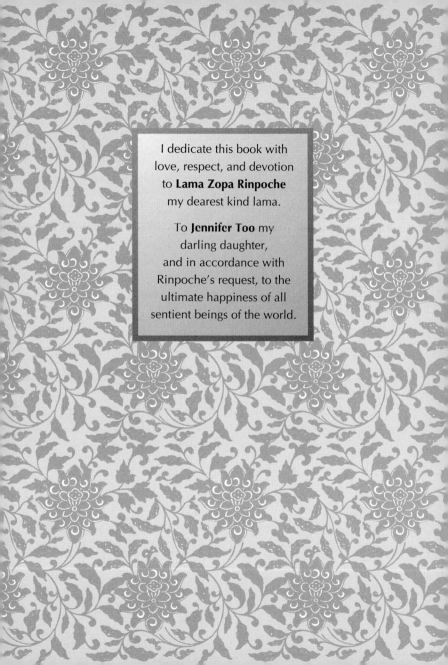

I dedicate this book with
love, respect, and devotion
to **Lama Zopa Rinpoche**
my dearest kind lama.

To **Jennifer Too** my
darling daughter,
and in accordance with
Rinpoche's request, to the
ultimate happiness of all
sentient beings of the world.

Feng Shui
Fundamentals

Love

Lillian Too

ELEMENT

Shaftesbury, Dorset • Boston, Massachusetts • Melbourne, Victoria

© Element Books Limited 1997
Text © Lillian Too 1997

First published in Great Britain by
ELEMENT BOOKS LIMITED
Shaftesbury, Dorset SP7 8BP

Published in the USA in 1997 by
ELEMENT BOOKS INC.
160 North Washington Street,
Boston, MA 02114

Published in Australia in 1997 by
ELEMENT BOOKS LIMITED
and distributed by Penguin Australia Ltd
487 Maroondah Highway, Ringwood, Victoria 3134
Reprinted 1998

Designed and created with
THE BRIDGEWATER BOOK COMPANY LIMITED

ELEMENT BOOKS LIMITED
Editorial Director Julia McCutchen
Managing Editor Caro Ness
Production Director Roger Lane
Production Sarah Golden

THE BRIDGEWATER BOOK COMPANY LIMITED
Art Director Terry Jeavons
Designer James Lawrence
Managing Editor Anne Townley
Project Editor Andrew Kirk
Editor Linda Doeser
Picture Research Julia Hanson
Studio Photography Guy Ryecart
Illustrations Isabel Rayner, Andrew Kulman, Mark Jamieson,
Michaela Blunden, Paul Collicutt, Olivia Rayner, Jackie Harland

Printed and bound in Hong Kong

British Library Cataloguing in Publication Data available

Library of Congress Cataloging in Publication data available

ISBN 1 86204 116 4

The publishers wish to thank the following for the use of pictures:
Elizabeth Whiting Associates, pp 27, 39; e.t. archive, p 9; Julia Hanson, p 41; Rex, p 46;
and Zefa, pp 13, 14, 15, 16, 17, 20, 31, 40, 45.

Special thanks go to:
Bright Ideas, Lewes, East Sussex
for help with properties

Lillian Too may be contacted on :
The World Wide Web
URL http://www.asiaconnect.com.my/lillian-too

Lillian Too's E-mail
ltoo@asiaconnect.com.my
ltoo@jaring.com.my

CONTENTS

WHAT IS FENG SHUI?

INTRODUCTION

風
水

Feng shui is a body of knowledge that offers specific methods for arranging and orienting homes, doors, furniture, and objects so that the living space is always conducive to the attraction of good fortune luck.

An ancient Chinese practice, its central tenet focuses on capturing auspicious luck from the earth by living in harmony with the natural energy forces that exist in the environment. Feng shui is currently enjoying a worldwide renaissance, and in recent years, the well-kept secrets of this science have become increasingly available, as many old texts on the practice are translated and aging Masters part with their valued formulas.

Feng shui's distinctive philosophy advocates arranging the living and work space in a way that allows residents to benefit from auspicious energy lines that run through the environment. These energies are called sheng chi, or, more lyrically, the dragon's cosmic breath.

Feng shui also offers guidelines on how to be aware of, and deal with, what is referred to as shar chi, or the secret killing breath that also lurks in the environment. These are harmful energy lines that bring bad luck, loss, disease, and misfortune.

The dragon features prominently in the language of feng shui. Excellent feng shui is said to be the result of the dragon's benign breath, and tapping into this cosmic breath is the best way to arrange one's living space.

THE PROMISE OF FENG SHUI

The promise of feng shui is exciting because it suggests that our material well-being and happiness can be enhanced simply by arranging objects in the living space according to its simple principles. There is feng shui advice to take care of every one of the basic aspirations of mankind: an improved income and the attainment of wealth, the enjoyment of good health and longevity, the development of a good education and successful career, the gaining of respect, recognition and even fame, getting help from friends and influential people, and the creation of a family unit that brings contentment and happiness.

Feng shui can also bring intense personal happiness in the form of excellent love and romance luck, thereby assisting people to achieve fulfillment in their marriage or in their romantic relationships. Feng shui addresses the universal need for love and offers guidelines that enable anyone to tap into auspicious energies that bring romance into life, improve the prospects for love and lasting relationships, and even save floundering marriages!

Feng shui fundamentals comprise a mixture of Chinese folk wisdom and special concepts that relate to yin and yang cosmology, Taoist philosophy, the five elements and their cycles of production and destruction, the trigrams of the I Ching arranged around the Pa Kua (the eight-sided symbol of feng shui), and the interplay of numbers in the magic Lo Shu square. The origins of feng shui go back thousands of years, but its principles are as effective today as then.

This ancient knowledge that has been handed down from generation to generation offers modern practitioners suggestions on the orientation and placement of objects within the home to enhance every kind of luck. This book is a practical guide offering the methods used to activate luck in romance and love, using both the form school (which is concerned with the landscape) and the compass school, which uses personalized formulas.

Following the principles of feng shui means that you are living in harmony with the cosmic dragon.

THE CHINESE VIEW
OF LOVE AND ROMANCE

The Chinese view lasting relationships as the ultimate in double happiness. Satisfaction in love and love-making is considered a principal ingredient of a worthy and successful life. To the Chinese, a happy love life adds to health and longevity, and feng shui directly addresses this dimension of living by offering various suggestions for improving our chances of attaining this happiness. This book addresses this aspect of feng shui and explains how to energize love, romance, and marriage luck.

In the past, however, the Chinese did not necessarily confine themselves to monogamous marriages; men often had several wives. For the young women of those times, enjoying auspicious luck in love was often synonymous with being the major wife, or "number one wife," of a successful husband and becoming the ruling matriarch of a household that included concubines and secondary wives. Translated for the 20th century, this means the practice of feng shui must be finely tuned to ensure that husbands and lovers stay faithful.

In the past, young men were thought to be lucky in love if they succeeded in marrying a suitably understanding first wife who conformed to the mores of the times. Indeed, as recently as the early part of this century, there were Chinese matri-

archs – even those living in Singapore and Malaysia – who accepted the presence of secondary wives in their household. My grandmother, for instance, allowed a young girl to share my grandfather's bedroom when she decided to retire from motherhood. I have uncles and aunts born of this secondary union, but my grandmother never lost her premier status within the household. It is important to take account of this aspect of traditional Chinese attitudes when using feng shui in a modern context.

In the past, eligible young men and women were brought together by a matchmaker. Good feng shui ensured a good match, which was defined as one that resulted in the creation of harmonious family luck. This, in turn, resulted in many sons, and happiness for the bride with her in-laws, leading to good treatment toward her and her children. In a modern context, this is also true: good marriage luck brings a match that makes everyone happy.

When we speak of activating romance luck using feng shui, we are, therefore, speaking of energizing our matrimonial and relationship luck. Feng shui can be used to enhance relationship prospects and bring about happiness and mutual respect. It does not promise fidelity within the marriage or relationship, but it can enhance and strengthen the family unit and, by so doing, offer harmony and peace within the home.

In the past, the emphasis of marriage
was on creating a strong family unit.
Traditionally feng shui has addressed
this aspect of marriage, but it can
also be adapted to modern couples
who expect loving and fulfilling
relationships within marriage.

THE PRINCIPLE OF
YIN AND YANG IN ROMANCE

The principle of yin and yang, which symbolizes the complementarity of opposing energies, exerts significant influence in the practice of feng shui. Yin and yang are primordial forces that represent male and female, light and dark, positive and negative, day and night, the sun and the moon – one gives existence and meaning to the other. Note that without light, there cannot be darkness, and without warmth, there cannot be cold.

In the same way, without male, there cannot be female and vice versa. To attain the supreme happiness of the whole, the philosophy pronounces that yin and yang, the female and male energies, must exist in harmony. Too much of one element or the other causes imbalance, which leads to unhappiness and, eventually, to bad luck and misfortune.

Balancing yin and yang forces in a relationship between two people suggests that both the male and female energies must be in harmony. Thus, fiery passion must be balanced with a certain coolness, assertiveness must be countered with receptivity, and strength with weakness. Only then can there be harmony. Where one leads, the other follows: there cannot be two leaders, otherwise the relationship will be too yang. Similarly, there cannot be two followers, for such a relationship will be too yin. Both situations are unbalanced and, thus, inauspicious.

There is always a little bit of yin in yang and vice versa and they continually interact, thereby creating the dynamics of change. When there is good balance between two people, each alternating

For romance to flourish there must be a balance between female yin and male yang energies.

up, good romance feng shui will enhance their chances of finding suitable partnerships that develop into happy, fruitful marriages or relationships. In this way, the whole cycle of life will continue down through the generations.

Good relationship and marriage feng shui is created when the relevant living space benefits from the auspicious breath of the dragon and when killing energies, caused by offensive structures and symbols, are completely eliminated or deflected from it.

The principle of yin and yang harmony is interwoven with other feng shui fundamentals to stimulate romance luck. You can add spice to your love life, improve your chances of meeting the right partner, even restore a flagging marriage by applying the guidelines contained in this book. There are various ways to activate good fortune in love; select those that can most easily be applied to your home or your room, if that better represents your personal living space.

Remember that in feng shui, more is not necessarily better. You do not need to use every single method contained in this book. Often, using one method correctly is sufficient to change or improve your luck.

between yin and yang roles as the relationship progresses, then there will be continuous harmony that leads to good fortune. Achieving this balance between husband and wife and between young couples is what romance feng shui teaches us. When the children of the family grow

ROMANCE FENG SHUI

USING THE PA KUA

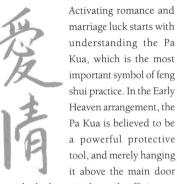

Activating romance and marriage luck starts with understanding the Pa Kua, which is the most important symbol of feng shui practice. In the Early Heaven arrangement, the Pa Kua is believed to be a powerful protective tool, and merely hanging it above the main door outside the home is deemed sufficient to deflect any negative energies that may be threatening the home and the members of the household.

However, the Pa Kua, with its aggregated circles of meanings, is also a reference tool for analysis. There is deep meaning in each of the symbols around the edge of it. In addition, each corner of this eight-sided emblem is designated by a trigram and each of these offers a wealth of meanings for feng shui interpretation. Trigrams are three-lined symbols; the lines may be solid, yang lines or broken, yin lines. The relationship of these lines is what gives meanings to the trigrams, according to the I Ching.

THE DIRECTION SOUTH-WEST

The trigram that represents love and relationships is the yin trigram Kun and, according to the Later Heaven Arrangement of trigrams, this is placed in the south-west. This is the corner of

any home or room that represents romance, love, and marriage. If this corner has good feng shui, the marriage and love aspirations of the members of the household will be positively energized.

If this corner has bad feng shui, however, bad marriage luck will befall the household, leading to divorce, loneliness, unhappiness, and an almost total absence of marriage opportunities for the sons and daughters of the family. Thus romance feng shui should always start with an examination of this sector of the room or home.

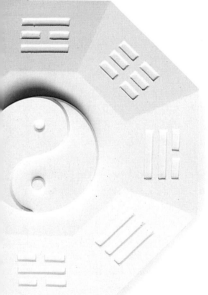

The Later Heaven Arrangement of trigrams is used inside the home.

KUN

 This trigram is made up of three broken yin lines. Kun is the trigram that symbolizes mother earth. Inherent to this trigram is the concept of the ideal matriarch, all that is receptive and ultimate yin energy. Kun symbolizes the person who accepts all the responsibilities of the family, performing the crucial role of keeping the family together, giving birth, raising children, and dispensing love and kindness, in spite of hard work. Like the earth, the matriarch grows everything and receives everything back. The earth supports mountains, cradles the oceans, and is always enduring. This is a powerful trigram. One of the best representations of it is a mountain, and a painting of mountains hung in the Kun corner brings extraordinary romantic luck.

PRODUCTIVE CYCLE

This illustration shows the productive cycle of the five elements - earth, metal, water, wood, and fire. Fire, the element that produces earth, is in a positive position in relation to earth and is therefore helping to energize earth, which is associated with love and marriage.

APPLYING FIVE ELEMENT ANALYSIS

The best method of energizing the southwest, thereby activating romance luck, is to apply the rationale of the five elements. According to the classical texts, all things in the universe, tangible or intangible, belong to one of five elements. These are fire, wood, water, metal, and earth and they are said to interact in never-ending productive and destructive cycles. Applying element analysis to feng shui requires an understanding of how the cycles work and how they may be applied in a practical way.

THE SIGNIFICANCE OF THE ELEMENT CYCLES

The element of the southwest corner is earth, symbolized by crystals, stones, boulders, and all things from the ground. Identifying the relevant element to activate is a vital part of the application. It suggests that placing, for instance, a boulder in the southwest corner of the garden will activate excellent romance and marriage opportunities for the residents of the house. From the cycles shown above, you will see several other attributes of the earth element.

DESTRUCTIVE CYCLE

This illustration shows the destructive cycle of the five elements. Earth is being overwhelmed by wood, the element that destroys earth. This means that earth, which is associated with love and marriage, is not being strengthened.

▨ Earth is produced by fire, so fire is said to be good for it.

▨ Earth itself produces metal, so metal is said to exhaust it.

▨ Earth is destroyed by wood, so wood is said to be harmful to it.

▨ Earth destroys water, so it is said to overcome water.

From these attributes we know that to strengthen the element of the southwest we can use all objects that symbolize both the earth and the fire elements, but we should strenuously avoid anything belonging to the wood element. Delving deeper, we see that the southwest is represented by mother earth itself. This suggests that the spirit of the earth energy here is strong, powerful, and not easily overcome. Big earth also suggests the presence of gold or something precious within. Thus, it is beneficial to introduce all five elements into the corner to ensure the fullness of the mother earth.

Remember that balance is vital in feng shui, for love and romance as for anything else. All five elements add subtly to each other and, by introducing all of them to the Kun corner, subtle attributes of each of them all can be effectively utilized. The romance luck activated by these arrangements will have depth and substance. If what you desire is to find someone to share your life, the scope of luck sought becomes all important.

ENERGIZING THE EARTH ELEMENT

In feng shui, each of the five elements is activated when objects belonging to it are present. One of the best objects to use to energize the earth element of the southwest romance corner is a crystal, especially natural quartz crystal dug up from the earth.

CRYSTALS

Raw amethyst, quartz, or other natural crystals will be extremely harmonious with the southwest sector. In addition, other minerals and metals from the earth are effective, although the energies created by the display of crystals is particularly positive. If you like, you can also use artificial, manmade lead crystals, which may be paperweights or even good-fortune symbols fashioned out of crystal and displayed on your table top.

The facets of crystal and cut glass are especially potent when combined with light.

Crystal chandeliers are said to attract tremendous good luck. Hung in the southwest corner of a room, a chandelier brings wonderful romantic and relationship luck. Chandeliers made with faceted crystal balls are also suitable in other corners of a room.

When hung in the center of the house, they shower the home with extremely auspicious family luck. This is because the center of any home, the heart of the residence, is also signified by the earth element and should represent the area of maximum energy or chi concentration. For this reason, feng shui also warns against locating kitchens, store rooms, and toilets in the center of a home, because all of these destroy beneficial chi.

Natural quartz crystal and artificial crystal paperweights.

Crystal chandeliers, if you can afford them, make excellent feng shui energizers. The combination of crystal (earth element) and light (fire element) usually spells success and happiness.

If you cannot afford a chandelier, buy a few loose crystal balls and hang them near a light or on windows that are bathed with sunshine. This brings valuable yang energies into the home, sometimes causing the sunlight to break up into colorful rainbows.

OTHER GOOD-FORTUNE EARTH OBJECTS

Large, round decorative earthenware jars and pots are excellent for the southwest corners of rooms. Place peacock feathers, artificial silk flowers, or, better still, freshly cut flowers inside these jars. On no account display dried or dead flowers or plants, not even decorative driftwood. Dead wood and dried plants signify the death of a romantic relationship.

A globe is wonderfully symbolic of mother earth. This object has been found to be very effective for stimulating the southwest corners of rooms. Place it on a table top and activate it daily by spinning it round. This creates wonderful yang energy that balances the yin of the southwest corner exceedingly well.

Any decorated pot or stone jar will activate the earth element in the romance corner.

COLORS

The earth element is also activated by using earth tones and hues and so curtains, duvets, carpets, and wallpaper in the southwest should contain predominantly earth colors. You can be as creative as you like when implementing the suggestions here, and they are by no means exclusive. Some people use paintings of mountain scenery to activate this corner. Whatever you use, however, do not overdo it. Stay balanced. In feng shui, less is often better than more.

A SPECIAL TIP

A tip for energizing the southwest corner, to attract suitable partners for grown-up daughters, is to place pebbles inside a shallow glass or crystal bowl, fill it with water, float some flowers on top, if you have any and place a floating candle in the center. This brings together a basket of elements and lighting the candle each day will attract vital energy to the corner. If you use flowers, change both them and the water daily. You can use pebbles of any color. Mix the colors if you wish.

Earth colored soft furnishings are used to activate the earth element.

USING OBJECTS OF THE FIRE ELEMENT

Applying the theory of the productive cycle of the elements, we also note that fire produces earth, so fire element features can also activate the southwest to energize marriage and relationship luck. For the Chinese, the color red, which is of the fire element, represents happiness, festivity, and celebrations. This is evident at Chinese weddings, where the bride always wears red.

The bride is wearing red, the color that symbolizes happiness and celebration.

The southwest sector of any room can also be favorably stimulated by locating the fireplace in this corner. This will be a powerful activator, particularly during the cold winter months when the fire burns and brings welcome warmth and good cheer into the home.

EARTH AND FIRE

Both earth and fire motifs can be painted or stenciled onto the southwest walls of your living room or incorporated into wall designs or soft furnishings.

Lights are another potent feng shui tool that can be used to manipulate the balance of elements. Always make sure that there is a bright light in the southwest corner. Keeping the corner well lit prevents the energies there from getting stale, and the favorable chi thus created will never become stagnant.

The element of the southwest corner, which represents love is earth, and earth motifs are placed to activate romantic relationships.

The sun motif is a powerful symbol of the fire element and, when placed in the southwest, it complements the earth element admirably.

The love knot worked in red is extremely effective when used for the southwest corner. It was a great favorite with Chinese ladies of an earlier era. The knot does not have an end and it appears to go on forever and is a symbol of undying love.

INDIVIDUAL MARRIAGE ORIENTATIONS

THE COMPASS FORMULA

方位

Your marriage and family direction, based on your date of birth, can be calculated using a potent compass feng shui formula. The formula was a closely guarded secret for many years and it is derived from the two principal symbols of feng shui – the eight-sided Pa Kua, with its layers of meanings, and the Lo Shu magic square, a nine-sector grid that further unlocks the secrets of the ancient Pa Kua.

Also known as the Pa Kua Lo Shu formula (Kua formula for short), this method of investigating personal marriage and family luck orientations was given to the author's feng shui Master by an old Taiwan feng shui Grand Master, who was a legend in his time. According to the feng shui Masters, the family direction can be activated to attract excellent relationship luck within the family, not just between husband and wife, but also between parents and children. Couples having problems conceiving children can also use this formula to orient their sleeping directions, thereby correcting the problem. Most of all, however, the formula is especially useful for ensuring that husbands and wives stay happily together.

If your Kua number is:

1 east group

2 west group

3 east group

4 east group

5 west group

6 west group

7 west group

8 west group

9 east group

THE KUA FORMULA

To determine your family and marriage orientation, first determine your Kua number. Obtain your Chinese year of birth based on the calendar on pages 24–25 and use the following calculation to get your Kua number. If you get number 5, which is not used in the Kua formula, follow number 2 if you are male and 8 if you are female.

Your Marriage/Family orientation is:

SOUTH for both males and females

NORTHWEST for both males and females

SOUTHEAST for both males and females

EAST for both males and females

NORTHWEST for males and **WEST** for females

SOUTHWEST for both males and females

NORTHEAST for both males and females

WEST for both males and females

NORTH for both males and females

THE KUA FORMULA

Add the last two digits of your Chinese year of birth. e.g. **1978**, 7+8=15
If the sum is higher than ten, always reduce to a single digit, thus 1+5=6

Males	**Females**
Subtract from	Add
10	**5**
thus	thus
10-6	**5+6**
=4	**=11**
So, for men born in	1+1=2
1978	So, for women born in
the Kua number is	**1978**
4	the Kua number is
	2

Now check against this table for your marriage and family direction and lucky Lo Shu number.

THE CHINESE CALENDAR

For the Chinese, the New Year begins in either late January or early February. When calculating your Kua number take note of this. Thus if you were born in January 1946 before the New Year, your Chinese year of birth is said to be 1945 and not 1946. This calendar also indicates the ruling element of your year of birth. This gives you further clues on which corner of the home, will have the most effect on your well-being.

Year	From	To	Element	Year	From	To	Element
1900	31 Jan 1900	18 Feb 1901	Metal	1923	16 Feb 1923	4 Feb 1924	Water
1901	19 Feb 1901	17 Feb 1902	Metal	1924	5 Feb 1924	24 Jan 1925	Wood
1902	18 Feb 1902	28 Jan 1903	Water	1925	25 Jan 1925	12 Feb 1926	Wood
1903	29 Jan 1903	15 Jan 1904	Water	1926	13 Feb 1926	1 Feb 1927	Fire
1904	16 Feb 1904	3 Feb 1905	Wood	1927	2 Feb 1927	22 Jan 1928	Fire
1905	4 Feb 1905	24 Jan1906	Wood	1928	23 Jan 1928	9 Feb 1929	Earth
1906	25 Jan 1906	12 Feb 1907	Fire	1929	10 Feb 1929	29 Jan 1930	Earth
1907	13 Feb 1907	1 Feb 1908	Fire	1930	30 Jan 1930	16 Feb 1931	Metal
1908	2 Feb 1908	21 Jan 1909	Earth	1931	17 Feb 1931	15 Feb 1932	Metal
1909	22 Jan 1909	9 Feb 1910	Earth	1932	16 Feb 1932	25 Jan 1933	Water
1910	10 Feb 1910	29 Jan 1911	Metal	1933	26 Jan 1933	13 Feb 1934	Water
1911	30 Jan 1911	17 Feb 1912	Metal	1934	14 Feb 1934	3 Feb 1935	Wood
1912	18 Feb 1912	25 Feb 1913	Water	1935	4 Feb 1935	23 Jan 1936	Wood
1913	26 Feb 1913	25 Jan 1914	Water	1936	24 Jan 1936	10 Feb 1937	Fire
1914	26 Jan 1914	13 Feb 1915	Wood	1937	11 Feb 1937	30 Jan 1938	Fire
1915	14 Feb 1915	2 Feb 1916	Wood	1938	31 Jan 1938	18 Feb 1939	Earth
1916	3 Feb 1916	22 Jan 1917	Fire	1939	19 Feb 1939	7 Feb 1940	Earth
1917	23 Jan 1917	10 Feb 1918	Fire	1940	8 Feb 1940	26 Jan 1941	Metal
1918	11 Feb 1918	31 Jan 1919	Earth	1941	27 Jan 1941	14 Feb 1942	Metal
1919	1 Feb 1919	19 Feb 1920	Earth	1942	15 Feb 1942	24 Feb 1943	Water
1920	20 Feb 1920	7 Feb 1921	Metal	1943	25 Feb 1943	24 Jan 1944	Water
1921	8 Feb 1921	27 Jan 1922	Metal	1944	25 Jan 1944	12 Feb 1945	Wood
1922	28 Jan 1922	15 Feb 1923	Water	1945	13 Feb 1945	1 Feb 1946	Wood

Year	From	To	Element	Year	From	To	Element
1946	2 Feb 1946	21 Jan 1947	Fire	1977	18 Feb 1977	6 Feb 1978	Fire
1947	22 Jan 1947	9 Feb 1948	Fire	1978	7 Feb 1978	27 Jan 1979	Earth
1948	10 Feb 1948	28 Jan 1949	Earth	1979	28 Jan 1979	15 Feb 1980	Earth
1949	29 Jan 1949	16 Feb 1950	Earth	1980	16 Feb 1980	4 Feb 1981	Metal
1950	17 Feb 1950	5 Feb 1951	Metal	1981	5 Feb 1981	24 Jan 1982	Metal
1951	6 Feb 1951	26 Jan 1952	Metal	1982	25 Jan 1982	12 Feb 1983	Water
1952	27 Jan 1952	13 Feb 1953	Water	1983	13 Feb 1983	1 Feb 1984	Water
1953	14 Feb 1953	2 Feb 1954	Water	1984	2 Feb 1984	19 Feb 1985	Wood
1954	3 Feb 1954	23 Jan 1955	Wood	1985	20 Feb 1985	8 Feb 1986	Wood
1955	24 Jan 1955	11 Feb 1956	Wood	1986	9 Feb 1986	28 Jan 1987	Fire
1956	12 Feb 1956	30 Jan 1957	Fire	1987	29 Jan 1987	16 Feb 1988	Fire
1957	31 Jan 1957	17 Feb 1958	Fire	1988	17 Feb 1988	5 Feb 1989	Earth
1958	18 Feb 1958	7 Feb 1959	Earth	1989	6 Feb 1989	26 Jan 1990	Earth
1959	8 Feb 1959	27 Jan 1960	Earth	1990	27 Jan 1990	14 Feb 1991	Metal
1960	28 Jan 1960	14 Feb 1961	Metal	1991	15 Feb 1991	3 Feb 1992	Metal
1961	15 Feb 1961	4 Feb 1962	Metal	1992	4 Feb 1992	22 Jan 1993	Water
1962	5 Feb 1962	24 Jan 1963	Water	1993	23 Jan 1993	9 Feb 1994	Water
1963	25 Jan 1963	12 Feb 1964	Water	1994	10 Feb 1994	30 Jan 1995	Wood
1964	13 Feb 1964	1 Feb 1965	Wood	1995	31 Jan 1995	18 Feb 1996	Wood
1965	2 Feb 1965	20 Jan 1966	Wood	1996	19 Feb 1996	7 Feb 1997	Fire
1966	21 Jan 1966	8 Feb 1967	Fire	1997	8 Feb 1997	27 Jan 1998	Fire
1967	9 Feb 1967	29 Jan 1968	Fire	1998	28 Jan 1998	15 Feb 1999	Earth
1968	30 Jan 1968	16 Feb 1969	Earth	1999	16 Feb 1999	4 Feb 2000	Earth
1969	17 Feb 1969	5 Feb 1970	Earth	2000	5 Feb 2000	23 Jan 2001	Metal
1970	6 Feb 1970	26 Jan 1971	Metal	2001	24 Jan 2001	11 Feb 2002	Metal
1971	27 Jan 1971	15 Feb 1972	Metal	2002	12 Feb 2002	31 Jan 2003	Water
1972	16 Feb 1972	22 Feb 1973	Water	2003	1 Feb 2003	21 Jan 2004	Water
1973	23 Feb 1973	22 Jan 1974	Water	2004	22 Jan 2004	8 Feb 2005	Wood
1974	23 Jan 1974	10 Feb 1975	Wood	2005	9 Feb 2005	28 Jan 2006	Wood
1975	11 Feb 1975	30 Jan 1976	Wood	2006	29 Jan 2006	17 Feb 2007	Fire
1976	31 Jan 1976	17 Feb 1977	Fire	2007	18 Feb 2007	6 Feb 2008	Fire

APPLYING THE KUA FORMULA IN THE HOME

Once you know your personal marriage direction, there are several ways you can match your individual energies with that of your environment. You can stimulate chi to your benefit.

Your Kua number offers you your most auspicious direction for safeguarding your personal happiness. It also identifies your luckiest compass location to ensure happiness in your love life. The luck referred to here is marriage and family relationship luck. When you activate your personal family direction and location, you would be effectively supplementing and enhancing your relationship luck.

HOW TO DO IT

The layout of your home should be demarcated into nine sectors according to the Lo Shu grid, as shown. To do this accurately, use a good compass (any Western compass will do) and, standing in the center of the home, identify the locations and divide the total floor space into nine equal grids. This is shown in the diagram opposite.

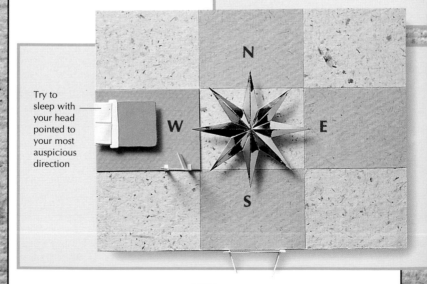

Try to sleep with your head pointed to your most auspicious direction

Nine equal grids.

YOUR BEDROOM

Try to locate your bedroom in your marriage and family location and to sleep with your head pointed to your marriage and family direction. If your direction is west, as shown here, this is where your bedroom should be located and the direction in which your bed should be pointed.

Your bed should be pointing toward your personal marriage direction to ensure happiness in love and marriage.

IRREGULAR-SHAPED HOMES

Houses and apartments seldom have regular, square, or rectangular shapes, making it difficult to superimpose a nine-sector grid on to the layout. More serious, however, is the problem of missing corners. If your marriage and family corner is missing as a result of the shape of your home, then your chances of enjoying good marriage and family luck are seriously undermined.

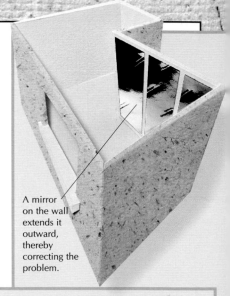

A mirror on the wall extends it outward, thereby correcting the problem.

THE SLEEPING DIRECTION

This is one of the most vital determinants of happiness within a marriage or love relationship. Try to sleep with your head pointed to your personal best direction for activating this aspect of your luck. The way to orient your bed is shown here. Let your head point in the direction desired (shown with arrows). This ensures that each night, even as you sleep, good luck chi is entering your body through your head.

IRREGULAR HOUSE SHAPES

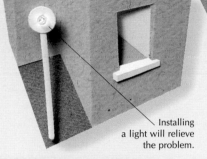

Installing a light will relieve the problem.

Building an extension is the best cure, but this depends on the space available.

There are ways of dealing with asymmetric rooms or houses and these are shown here, but correcting the problem merely improves the situation. It does not create the auspicious luck you would want.

According to feng shui, missing corners mean the home will be lacking in certain luck aspects. What types of luck are missing depend on the corresponding compass directions of missing sectors. If one missing sector represents your marriage and family direction, you can partially correct the matter by one of the following methods.

▒ Install a light.
▒ Hang a mirror on the wall.
▒ Build an extension.

What you do depends on your circumstances and whether you have the available space.

An irregular-shaped house layout sometimes makes it difficult to have the bedroom located, or your bed oriented, in the most auspicious way. If you cannot get the location you want for your bedroom, tapping the marriage direction alone is often good enough to improve things.

If you cannot tap either the location or direction, try, at least, to sleep with your head pointed to at least to one of your other auspicious directions (see pages 30–31). Remember that the sleeping direction refers to the direction where the top of the head points.

EAST AND WEST GROUP DIRECTIONS

Compass feng shui divides the human race into either east or west group people. Every person has four auspicious directions, with each one representing a different kind of luck. Thus, in addition to the good fortune marriage and family direction, you will have three other beneficial directions. These other auspicious directions depend on whether you are an east or a west group person which, in turn, depends on your Kua number.

●

East group people have Kua numbers one, three, four, and nine. East group directions are east, north, south, and southeast.

●

West group people have Kua numbers two, five, six, seven, and eight. West group directions are west, southwest, northwest and northeast.

●

East group directions do not bode well for west group people and vice versa. Try at all costs to have the main entrance to your home facing one of your auspicious directions.

EATING AND SLEEPING WITH LOVE IN MIND

Armed with your personal marriage and family direction, you can begin to activate it to enhance your love life. This is done by consciously arranging your sitting orientation within the home and each time you are out on a date with someone important to you. Always sit down to a meal with the one you love facing your own direction. This is easier than it sounds. Simply keep a pocket compass with you at all times in order to ascertain the direction in which you are facing. This is necessary because feng shui becomes most potent when personalized directions are activated.

However, it is equally essential to observe several important rules that are part of general form school feng shui guidelines. It is vital to point out here that no matter how well you may have oriented your beds, chairs, and other furniture in the home, if you inadvertently get hit by the pernicious killing breath caused by offensive structures within your immediate

vicinity, the killing breath prevails over the good feng shui. Similarly, there are important feng shui taboos to bear in mind. These are easy to detect and deal with, once you have been made aware of them in the following pages.

When having a meal together, be sure to sit with the person you love facing your personal marriage and family direction.

INSIDE THE BEDROOM

While it is ideal to have a regular-shaped bedroom located in the part of the home that corresponds to your marriage and family direction, this is not always possible. You should try very hard to have your head pointed in your personal direction. If you cannot do this make sure you do not have it pointed toward any of your four inauspicious directions. Select one of the other three that is suitable for you.

TABOOS TO BE OBSERVED AND AVOIDED

Never sleep with a mirror facing your bed. A television is regarded as being the same as a mirror, as it also reflects your image. If you do have a tele-vision in the bedroom, make sure you cover it when it is not in use. A mirror in the bedroom is one of the most harmful feng shui features. Mirrors facing the bed, in reflecting the couple, suggest interfer-ence from outside and consequently a marriage or relationship may fall apart through infidelity. If you want to have a harmonious relationship with your loved one, you are strongly advised to cover up mirrors installed on closet doors and to move your dressing table – with its inevitable mirror – into another room.

Never sleep under an exposed, overhead beam. The severity of the adverse effect depends on where the beam crosses the bed. If it cuts the bed in half, in addition to causing severe headaches, it also symbolically separates the couple sleeping underneath. If the beam is pressing on the heads of the couple, it will cause petty disagreements that develop into severe quarrels. If it is by the side of the bed, the effect is lessened. If your bed is affected by a beam, move the bed out of the way. If this is not possible, try to camouflage it in some way.

Never sleep on a bed placed directly in front of the door to the bedroom, irrespective of your sleeping direction. It does not matter whether your head or your feet point toward the door, this bed position is equally harmful. One or both members of the couple will suffer from ill health. There will be no time for love and health becomes a problem. Move the bed out of the way of the door or place some kind of divider in the way.

Never sleep with the sharp edge of a protruding corner pointed at you. This is a common problem. Many bedrooms have such corners and they are as harmful as pillars. The sharp edge of the corner is one of the most deadly forms of poison arrows that bring shar chi, or killing breath. The solution to this problem is to block off or camouflage the corner. Using plants is an ideal solution in the living room, but the presence of plants is not such a good idea in the bedroom. It is better to use a piece of furniture to conceal the sharp edge.

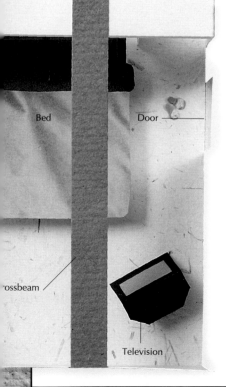

Bed

Door

Crossbeam

Television

This bedroom has a disastrous feng shui arrangement. The bed is being attacked by poison arrows, there is a television acting as a mirror, a crossbeam is pressing on the bed, and ill health is being invited in through the door.

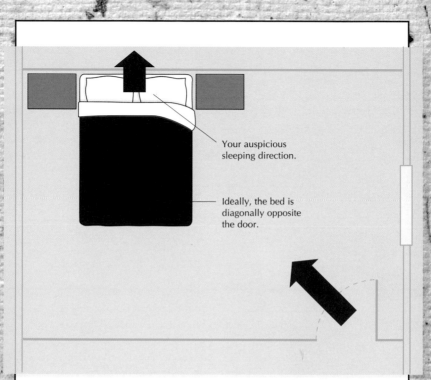

Your auspicious
sleeping direction.

Ideally, the bed is
diagonally opposite
the door.

LOCATION OF BEDS AND BEDROOMS

Make sure your bed is located in an auspicious place according to form school feng shui before attempting to tap your best personal direction. When using feng shui to enhance any aspect of your life or surroundings it is always advisable to start out by first protecting yourself from hidden poison arrows. Take care of any offensive features first before doing anything else. Next focus on the placement of the bed inside the room itself.

The arrow above shows you how to take the direction in the correct way. Note that it is the head that must be pointed in the direction you want. If you and your partner have different auspicious directions, sleep in two separate beds or let the direction of the breadwinner prevail. However, note that the bed is placed diagonally to the door. This is the best placement of the bed from a feng shui point of view.

EXAMPLES OF HARMFUL BED PLACEMENT

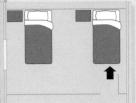

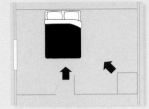

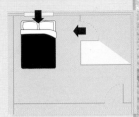

The bed placed directly in front of the door will suffer from bad chi. Note the direction of the arrow.

The bed is being hit by the sharp edge of the protruding corner as well as by the door. Move the bed and camouflage the offensive corner.

The bed is placed just below a window. It is also being hit by the door to the toilet in the en suite bathroom. These are both inauspicious features. The bed should be moved to the opposite corner.

EXAMPLES OF HARMFUL BEDROOM PLACEMENT

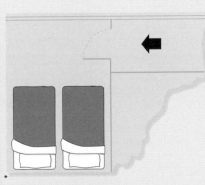

To safeguard the harmony of the home, the placement of the bedroom within the overall layout is also important. Try to select a bedroom that does not have any of the following features.

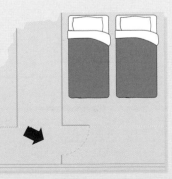

A bedroom located at the end of a long corridor is inauspicious. If the door to the bedroom opens directly to the corridor, the bad luck is more severe. Couples sleeping in such a bedroom will have no peace.

If the bedroom door is being hit by the edge of a another room in the home, the bedroom suffers from bad luck.

THE EFFECT OF TOILETS

In ancient China, the palaces and homes of wealthy Chinese did not have inside toilets. Slaves and servants brought in portable toilets and tubs of water for the master and mistress of the house to placed in any one of your auspicious locations, it destroys the specific luck represented by that location. Thus, if the toilet that is en suite in your bedroom is located in your marriage and family corner, it is harmful to your marriage luck,

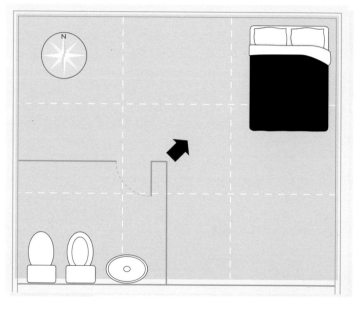

perform their ablutions – and removed them after use. In humbler households, toilets were located in sheds at some distance from the main house. This arrangement was based on the feng shui belief that toilets have an adverse effect on the fortunes of the residents.

Feng shui Masters of the Pa Kua Lo Shu school warn that when the toilet is

This bedroom has been divided into nine equal sectors to determine the location of the toilet. Notice that the toilet makes the room L-shaped and the edge of it sends killing breath toward the bed. The compass reading also indicates that the toilet is in the southwest corner, an inauspicious placement for relationships. If it is your personal family and marriage direction, the placement of this toilet is twice as harmful: either love will pass you by or you will encounter problems in your relationship.

A BED BESIDE A BATHROOM

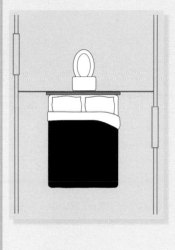

The bed should not be positioned against a wall with a toilet on the other side. This blocks the good energy from coming through.

OVERHEAD TOILET

The bed should not be placed immediately below a bathroom on the upper level, especially directly below the toilet. This oppresses the sleepers and results in a great deal of illness and misfortune.

causing distress and unhappiness in your marriage or love relationship. If the bedroom is occupied by a single person and the toilet is located in either the occupant's family and marriage location, or in the southwest (the universal romance corner applicable to everyone), then all opportunities for lasting relationships simply dry up.

Toilets are believed to create many inauspicious energies, and they should be kept closed when not in use. It is also a good idea to make sure that toilets are as small as possible, rather than going for the so-called spacious, luxurious look. Two other toilet orientations to be wary of in respect of the bed and bedroom are shown in the illustrations above.

LIGHTS

Lighting in the bedroom should be subdued rather than harsh. Spotlights are never recommended because the bedroom is a yin place. It is, however, necessary to guard against making the bedroom decor too yin. For example, blue lights with dark-colored bed sheets cause the yin energy to be excessive. Lights should merely be subdued. It is also necessary to guard against fittings and lamps that come in shapes that appear threatening.

Spotlights are unsuitable for bedrooms.

Tiffany lamps are far more suitable.

STAIRCASES

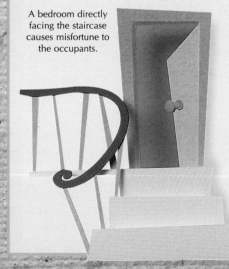

A bedroom directly facing the staircase causes misfortune to the occupants.

Bedrooms are also affected by the location of staircases relative to the door. Staircases that directly face the door of a bedroom cause the energy to be too strong. Bedrooms that have mezzanine floors that are accessed by a spiral staircase also suffer from grave misfortune because the staircase resembles a corkscrew boring in to the heart of the home.

PLANTS AND WATER IN THE BEDROOM

Plants are very effective energizers for certain corners of the bedroom, but they should be used with care. This is because the bedroom is a place for sleeping, where the yin energy prevails. Although it should not have an excess of yin energy, plants could be too yang, especially in a small bedroom. They denote life and growth – activity – and interfere with a good night's sleep.

Whilst water features are often used to activate the wealth or career sectors, they should be handled with extreme care in the bedroom, especially large aquariums or fish bowls placed behind or near the bed.

Plants denote yang energy and should not be placed in a small bedroom.

Spiral staircases may look good, but they are never recommended. They are especially harmful when located in the center of the home. They are not to be confused with curved staircases which are very auspicious.

Water features should be used with care in the bedroom as they may interfere with sleep.

BEDROOM FURNITURE

When things go wrong between you and your partner and keep going wrong for no apparent reason, when love seems suddenly to have faded and died, especially when you have recently redecorated your bedroom or just moved into a new home, it is a good idea to investigate the feng shui of the bedroom furniture. It is very likely you are being hit by shar chi, which is caused by any number of things. The most harmful of bedroom taboos – mirrors, beams, and corners – have already been featured, but there are less obvious feng shui problems that may be inadvertently caused by your choice of furniture in the bedroom or elsewhere in the house.

EFFECTS OF DIFFERENT SHAPED FURNITURE

Bookcases, display cabinets, and closets should have doors that cover the shelves within. Exposed shelves are like blades sending hostile energy into the room.

Closets and book shelves directly facing the bed should be made with closing doors. Exposed shelves create shar chi, causing those who sleep in the room to have headaches, migraine, and short temper. These shelves represent sharp knives sticking in to you. Use artificial creepers to blunt the edge of the shelves if there are no doors. Closets that face the bed should not have mirrored doors, since these also send malignant vibrations toward the bed, thereby affecting the sleeping couple.

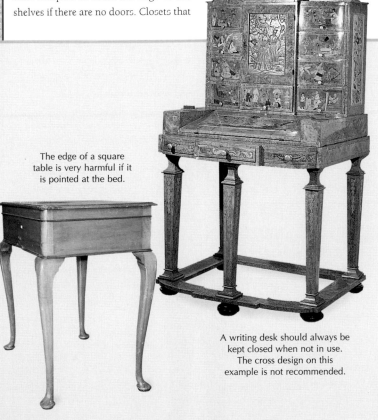

The edge of a square table is very harmful if it is pointed at the bed.

A writing desk should always be kept closed when not in use. The cross design on this example is not recommended.

ENHANCING YOUR MARRIAGE PROSPECTS

ACTIVATING YOUR MARRIAGE AND LOVE CORNER

For those keen on adding sparkle and new energy to their love lives and enhancing their marriage prospects, Kua formula feng shui offers some simple, yet effective, suggestions. While much of bedroom feng shui focuses on harnessing good fortune for those already married, combining the Kua formula with the use of good-fortune symbols can sometimes work wonders in bringing about a more active and enjoyable social and love life for single people.

HOW TO DO IT

▨ Check your personal marriage and family direction based on your Kua number (see pages 22–23).

▨ Select a room in your home that you wish to activate. It should be a room where you spend a great deal of time, but preferably not your bedroom. The living room or the study or work room is usually ideal.

▨ Stand in the center of the room and take your compass bearings. Identify the corner of the room that represents your marriage and family direction. Do this by superimposing an imaginary grid of nine sectors, then accurately mark out the sector that represents your marriage corner. This is the area of the room you will need to activate.

▨ Next, select from the good fortune symbols listed opposite. You can buy these items or make your own symbols.

If you have difficulty finding ducks, lovebirds are also excellent symbols of love. You can even keep live budgerigars in your love corner, but you should always keep them in a pair.

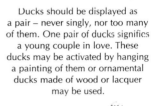

Ducks should be displayed as a pair – never singly, nor too many of them. One pair of ducks signifies a young couple in love. These ducks may be activated by hanging a painting of them or ornamental ducks made of wood or lacquer may be used.

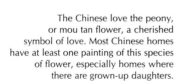

The Chinese love the peony, or mou tan flower, a cherished symbol of love. Most Chinese homes have at least one painting of this species of flower, especially homes where there are grown-up daughters.

SYMBOLS OF ROMANCE AND LOVE

The Chinese have several symbols that signify romance and conjugal happiness. Apart from the powerful double happiness symbol, which can be reproduced and hung on the wall, another wonderful object to display in your love corner is a pair of mandarin ducks.

Western symbols can also be used for romance luck – hearts, pictures of a bride and groom, wedding bouquets, and even paintings of lovers.

THE SIGNIFICANCE
OF THE MAIN DOOR DIRECTION

Using your Kua number, it is possible to investigate whether the main entrance into your home is auspicious for your love life. The following table summarizes the kind of chi energy affecting your life if your main entrance faces each of the eight directions indicated.

Main Door Directions

Kua No.	North	South	East	West	N-east	N-west	S-east	S-west
1	D	C	B	E	F	G	A	H
2	H	G	E	B	A	C	F	D
3	B	A	D	H	G	F	C	E
4	A	B	C	G	H	E	D	F
5 males	H	G	E	B	A	C	F	D
5 females	F	E	G	C	D	B	H	A
6	G	H	F	A	B	D	E	C
7	E	F	H	D	C	A	G	B
8	F	E	G	C	D	B	H	A
9	C	D	A	F	E	H	B	G

WHAT YOUR DOOR DIRECTION MEANS

A The home is conducive to attracting a close and loving relationship for the sons and daughters of the family and unions will generally be successful and happy. The home has auspicious marriage luck.

B Residents enjoy good family luck and marriages stay happy. There is also the promise of good health. Here the chi energies are benevolent.

C The chi energy is smooth and excellent. You will enjoy extremely good romance feng shui. Opportunities for meeting people abound and most of your relationships are happy ones.

D The chi energy is fluctuating. Romantic love is sometimes good and sometimes bad.

E The chi energy is uncertain and although there are opportunities, it is not certain that things will work out. Romance leads to heartbreak and there are trials and tribulations.

F The chi energy has become sour and bad. Unless great effort is expended, the luck is bad. Unions lead to failure. There is betrayal and unhappiness.

G The chi is suffocating. There will be severe health problems for both partners. Men will become ill, women may be unfaithful. The advice is to be wary.

H The chi is extremely unfortunate. It brings constant misunderstandings, severe quarrels, and, eventually, it could lead to loss, lawsuits, a great deal of unhappiness, and, sometimes, even death.

ADDITIONAL GUIDELINES

Guard your main door against being hit by shar chi from its immediate surroundings. Make sure it is not directly facing the following structures:

- A single large, tall tree.
- A tall building or wall.
- A neighbor's triangular roof line.
- A hospital, police station, or cemetery.
- A T-junction or a Y-junction.
- A gate, either your neighbor's or your own.
- A tall structure of any kind, such as a chimney, an electricity pylon, or a pillar.

If you live in an apartment building, the main door into the building is deemed to be your main door, but the door into your apartment is also important.

The direction of the main door will determine the type of love energy that enters your home.

CHECKING COMPATIBILITY

EAST AND WEST GROUP PEOPLE

相客

The Kua formula used in compass feng shui also offers one of the most accurate ways of investigating the degree of compatibility between two people. As a general rule, it is highly recommended that people should marry someone from the same group. When an east group person marries a west group person, the compatibility is seriously reduced and, depending on the individual Kua numbers of both, the incompatibility can be quite severe, sometimes so serious that both parties eventually end up harming each other. Perhaps the most famous case of this kind of incompatibility was the marriage between Britain's HRH Prince Charles and Princess Diana, which ended in separation and misery.

EXAMPLE

If your Kua number is three, then the best match for you will be someone with the Kua number one, your sheng chi. He or she will not only make you happy, but will also bring you luck. At the same time people with Kua numbers nine, three, and four are also compatible. Those with Kua number three, therefore, should be wary about becoming involved with people whose Kua numbers are other than those indicated.

COMPATIBLE KUA NUMBERS

Your Kua No.	Sheng Chi Kua	Tien Yi Kua	Nien Yen Kua	Fu Wei Kua
1	3	4	1	9
2	7	8 (m) 8&5 (f)	2&5 (m) 2 (f)	6
3	1	9	3	4
4	9	1	4	3
5	7 (m) 6 (f)	8 (m) 2 (f)	5	6 (m) 7 (f)
6	8 (m) 8&5 (f)	7	6	2&5 (m) 2 (f)
7	2&5 (m) 2 (f)	6	7	8 (m) 8&5 (f)
8	6	2&5 (m) 2 (f)	8 (m) 8&5 (f)	7
9	4	3	9	1

The table above indicates the degrees of compatibility between people of different Kua numbers. Use it to check the compatibility between you and your loved one. Remember that the key to unlocking the meanings lies in your Kua number which you can work out from the formula given on page 23.

Males with Kua number five should follow the numbers with (m) after and females with Kua number five should use the numbers with (f) after. The table refers to Kua numbers that are compatible to your Kua number. Note that east group people are always compatible with others of the east group and west group people with others of the west. The degree of compatibility is described as follows.

▨ Sheng Chi Kua: extremely compatible; your partner will bring you excellent luck.

▨ Tien Yi Kua: very compatible, your partner looks after your health well.

▨ Nien Yen Kua: extremely compatible; a most harmonious and happy relationship.

▨ Fu Wei Kua: very compatible; your partner is supportive and encouraging.

Your Kua No.	Ho Hai Kua	Wu Kwei Kua	Lui Sha Kua	Chueh Ming Kua
1	6	2&5 (m)	7	8&5 (f)
2	9	1	3	4
3	8&5 (m)	7	2&5 (m)	6
4	7	8&5 (f)	6	2&5 (m)
5	9 (m) 3 (f)	1 (m) 4 (f)	3 (m) 9 (f)	4 (m) 1 (f)
6	1	9	4	3
7	4	3	1	9
8	3	4	9	1
9	2&5 (m)	6	8&5 (f)	7

Males with Kua number five should follow the numbers with (m) after and females with Kua number five should follow the numbers with (f) after. The numbers in the table refer to Kua numbers that are incompatible with your Kua number. Note that east group people are incompatible with west group people and vice versa. These numbers refer only to Kua numbers and not anything else. The degree of incompatibility is described as follows.

▨ Ho Hai Kua: your partner will cause you accidents and mishaps. The relationship is not smooth.

▨ Wu Kwei Kua: very incompatible; both of you will quarrel constantly and there is anger in the relationship. This is the five ghosts relationship, suggesting that outside parties will succeed in causing problems between the two of you.

EXAMPLE

If your Kua number is eight, then your most dangerous match is someone with the Kua number one, which represents total loss for you, but Kua numbers nine, four, and three are also incompatible and best avoided. There can be no happiness in a long-term relationship with people who have these Kua numbers.

- ▨ Lui Sha Kua: extremely incompatible; your partner will cause you grievous harm and immense heartbreak. This is the six killings description, it is far better to part.
- ▨ Chueh Ming Kua: totally and irretrievably incompatible. Your partner will be the death of you, figuratively and metaphorically. He or she could ruin your name, cause you to lose wealth and break your heart totally. Avoid this partnerhsip at all costs.

OTHER SYSTEMS

The east and west group formula to determine compatibility between partners complements the astrological method, which uses the Chinese ghanzhi system of heavenly stems and earthly branches (see pages 50–51). This latter method is best known under the Chinese zodiac animal signs. In the old days, both these methods, as well as detailed astrological charts, were drawn up to investigate compatibility. On occasion, although the Kua formula and the ghanzhi system indicate compatibility, sometimes the elements (wood, fire, water, metal, and earth) of the birth charts seriously override the readings, causing problems between seemingly compatible couples. Similarly, the elements of the birth chart can also override seeming incompatibility, but again these are rare occurrences.

The five elements: fire, earth, metal, water, wood.

CHINESE ASTROLOGICAL COMPATIBILITY

In the Chinese astrological chart, there are 12 zodiac animals, each representing one year in a cycle of 12. These are referred to as the earthly branches. The 12-year cycles are repeated five times to represent the five elements: fire, wood, water, earth, and metal. These elements are designated as heavenly stems. Together this makes up a cycle of 60 years (12x5=60). This astrological arrangement is termed the ganzhi system.

Every lunar year is thus described in terms of branches and stems – animals and elements. The year 1997, for example, is the year of the ox, and the element is earth. You can work out your stem and branch combination from the calendar given on pages 24–5 and, using that information, you can undertake a compatibility check based on two methods.

- You can check the compatibility of your earthly branch – the animal compatibility.
- You can check the compatibility of your heavenly stems – the element compatibility.

CHECKING THE HEAVENLY STEMS

The productive and destructive cycles of the five elements (see pages 14–15) help to indicate a couple's compatibility or incompatibility.

CHECKING THE EARTHLY BRANCHES

Animals that belong to each of the four triangles of affinity (see diagram) are compatible, as follows.

- The competitors of the horoscope are the Rat, the Monkey and the Dragon. They get along famously.
- The independents are the Horse, the Dog, and the Tiger. They love each other.
- The intellectuals are the Snake, the Rooster, and the Ox. They have eyes only for each other.
- The diplomats are the Rabbit, the Sheep, and the Boar. They are wildly compatible!

All animals that are directly opposite each other (see diagram) are said to be incompatible. This means a six-year age gap is considered incompatible as follows:

- Rat and Horse
- Ox and Sheep
- Tiger and Monkey
- Rabbit and Rooster
- Dragon and Dog
- Snake and Boar

These combinations are incompatible as a couple. Although they can be good friends, these couples just cannot live together in harmony.

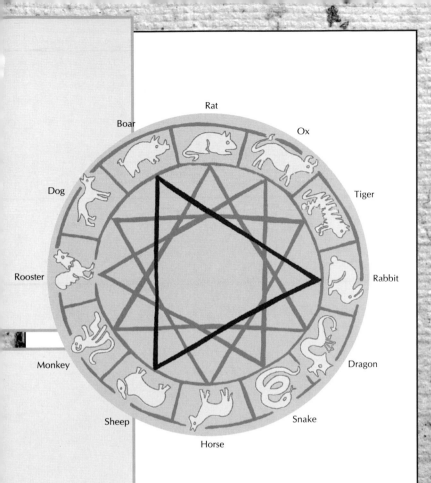

Rat

Boar

Ox

Dog

Tiger

Rooster

Rabbit

Monkey

Dragon

Sheep

Snake

Horse

Each year of the Chinese astrological cycle of 12 years is represented by an animal. The 12 animals run in sequence, beginning with the rat and followed by the ox, tiger, rabbit, dragon, snake, horse, sheep, monkey, rooster, dog, and lastly, the boar. Whatever year a person is born into determines their personality and physical being. It is important to check the compatibility or otherwise of any potential partner.

SPECIFIC FENG SHUI ADVICE FOR WOMEN

A TIP FOR THE MARRIED WOMAN

女性

It is important for women who practice feng shui to remember that this is an ancient science from China. In the past, feng shui was used to create wealth, success, happiness, and prominence for families, particularly the head of the family. Success for a man was often measured not just by his wealth and position, but also by the number of concubines and secondary wives that he had. Indeed, men of stature always had an entire harem of wives. Thus, when you introduce feng shui inspired changes to your house, particularly methods that involve the use of water (which signifies wealth), it is prudent to be very careful.

One of the most important tips passed onto me by a very knowledgeable feng shui Master skilled in the practice of water feng shui was that pools of water in the vicinity of homes should never be located on the right-hand side of the main front door. Whether the pool of water is inside or outside the house, it should always be placed on the left-hand

The water feature, left of the main door.

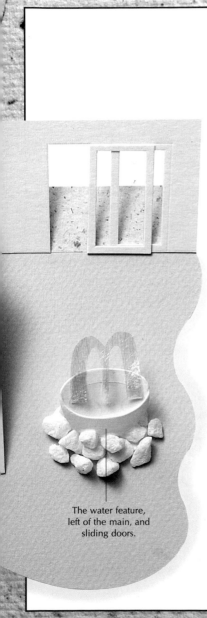

The water feature, left of the main, and sliding doors.

side of the front door. Otherwise, although your husband may be successful and indeed grow wealthy and prosperous, he will also develop a roving eye. At best, if your marriage feng shui has been correctly implemented, he will only look. At worst, however, he could well become unfaithful or leave you altogether.

Therefore, women should ensure that this particular guideline concerning water is scrupulously followed if they want to keep their husbands or partners faithful. The way to determine the location is to stand inside the house looking out. The pool or pond should then be placed on your left side.

Families lucky enough to have swimming pools in their gardens should be especially attentive to this guideline, since the same principle applies to a swimming pool as to any other pool of water. Is it any coincidence that so many successful men all over the world discard their wives after reaching the top?

If you already have a pond or a pool and it is located on the wrong side of your main door, my advice to the lady of the household is to move it, fill it in, or do away with it altogether!

The illustration shows two ponds, one inside the house and one outside. Both ponds are on the left-hand side of the doors – the main door, as well as the sliding doors by the side. Notice that the orientation is taken from inside the house.

TIPS FOR SINGLE PEOPLE SEEKING LOVE

There are two excellent methods for activating the romance corner of the garden – the southwest. These methods can be used by everyone and work just as well for men as for women. The effect is that you will succeed in attracting the right man or woman into your life. In the past, mothers, anxious for their sons and daughters to find good matches and produce heirs for the next generation, had a great deal of success with these methods.

CHANNELING THE EARTH ELEMENT WITH LIGHT

Use a long hollow rod made of copper or steel – the kind used for domestic plumbing is ideal. Place it in the ground, in the exact southwest corner of your garden, making sure it is at least 3ft (1m) deep. The rod taps into the energy of the earth. To make the earth chi rise up from the ground, place very bright lights at the top of the rod. Make sure that you keep the lights turned on for at least three hours each night.

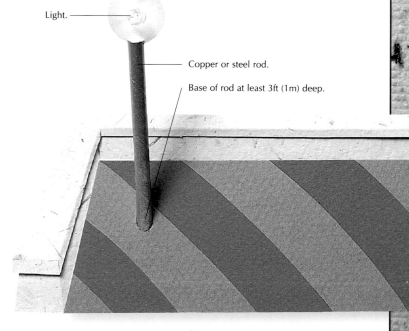

Light.

Copper or steel rod.

Base of rod at least 3ft (1m) deep.

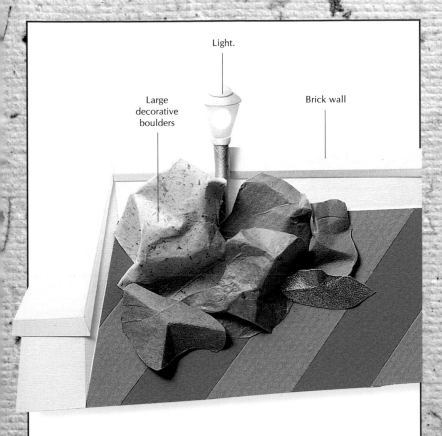

Light.

Large
decorative
boulders

Brick wall

STRENGTHENING THE
EARTH ELEMENT WITH BOULDERS

Once again locate the southwest corner of the garden accurately. A brick wall in that part of the garden is excellent, but it does not matter if you have not got one. Find two or three large, decorative boulders and arrange them in the southwest so that they form part of the garden landscape. These boulders repre-sent the earth element. To activate them and encourage the yang energy to rise, obtain some red rope and tie it round the boulder. According to feng shui, tying anything with red thread will always succeed in energizing it. If possible, have a light in the same corner. Strengthening the earth element activates the marriage corner encouraging lasting relationships for residents within the home.

INDEX

FURTHER READING

Kwok, Man-Ho and O'Brien, Joanne,
The Elements of Feng Shui,
ELEMENT BOOKS, SHAFTESBURY, 1991

Lo, Raymond *Feng Shui: The Pillars of
Destiny (Understanding Your Fate and
Fortune),* TIMES EDITIONS, SINGAPORE, 1995

Skinner, Stephen, *Living Earth Manual
of Feng Shui: Chinese Geomancy,*
PENGUIN, 1989

Too, Lillian, *The Complete Illustrated
Guide to Feng Shui,* ELEMENT BOOKS,
SHAFTESBURY, 1996

Too, Lillian *Basic Feng Shui,*
KONSEP BOOKS, KUALA LUMPUR, 1997

Too, Lillian *Chinese Astrology for Romance
and Relationships* , KONSEP BOOKS,
KUALA LUMPUR, 1996

Too, Lillian *Chinese Numerology
in Feng Shui,* KONSEP BOOKS,
KUALA LUMPUR, 1994

Too, Lillian *Dragon Magic,*
KONSEP BOOKS, KUALA LUMPUR, 1996

Too, Lillian *Feng Shui,* KONSEP BOOKS,
KUALA LUMPUR, 1993

Too, Lillian *Practical Applications for
Feng Shui,* KONSEP BOOKS, KUALA LUMPUR, 1994

Too, Lillian *Water Feng Shui for Wealth,*
KONSEP BOOKS, KUALA LUMPUR, 1995

Walters, Derek *Feng Shui Handbook:
A Practical Guide to Chinese Geomancy
and Environmental Harmony,*
AQUARIAN PRESS, 1991

USEFUL ADDRESSES

Feng Shui Design Studio
PO Box 705, Glebe, Sydney, NSW 2037,
Australia, Tel: 61 2 315 8258

Feng Shui Society of Australia
PO Box 1565, Rozelle, Sydney
NSW 2039, Australia

**The Geomancer
The Feng Shui Store**
PO Box 250, Woking, Surrey GU21 1YJ
Tel: 44 1483 839898
Fax: 44 1483 488998

Feng Shui Association
31 Woburn Place, Brighton BN1 9GA,
Tel/Fax: 44 1273 693844

Feng Shui Network International
PO Box 2133, London W1A 1RL,
Tel: 44 171 935 8935,
Fax: 44 171 935 9295

The School of Feng Shui
34 Banbury Road, Ettington,
Stratford-upon-Avon, Warwickshire
CV37 7SU. Tel/Fax: 44 1789 740116

The Feng Shui Institute of America
PO Box 488, Wabasso, FL 32970,
Tel: 1 407 589 9900 Fax: 1 407 589 1611

Feng Shui Warehouse
PO Box 3005, San Diego, CA 92163,
Tel: 1 800 399 1599 Fax: 1 800 997 9831

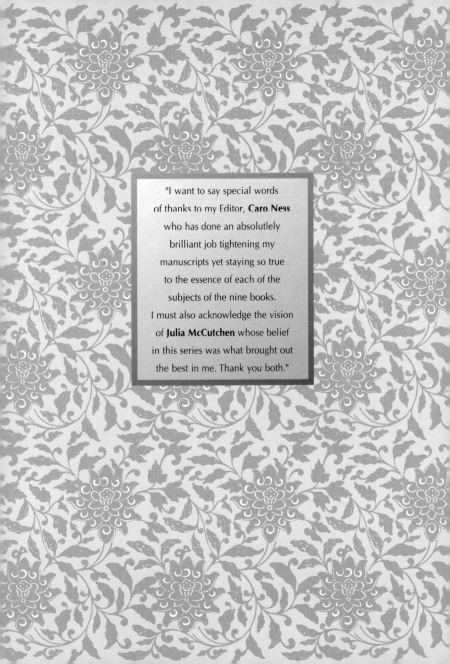

"I want to say special words of thanks to my Editor, **Caro Ness** who has done an absolutley brilliant job tightening my manuscripts yet staying so true to the essence of each of the subjects of the nine books. I must also acknowledge the vision of **Julia McCutchen** whose belief in this series was what brought out the best in me. Thank you both."

**Other titles in the
Feng Shui Fundamentals
series are:**

Careers
Children
Education
Eight Easy Lessons
Fame
Health
Networking
Wealth